MW00887073

COACHING YOUTH VOLLEYBALL

TABLE OF CONTENTS

TABLE OF CONTENTS

INTRODUCTION

Unlock the potential of young athletes and dive into the world of teamwork, skill development, and mentorship with 'Coaching Youth Volleyball.' This comprehensive guide is your essential companion to nurturing a love for the game while instilling valuable life lessons in the next generation of volleyball stars. Whether you're a seasoned coach or a newcomer to the sport, this book equips you with the knowledge and strategies to inspire and guide your team to success on and off the court.

THE ESSENTIAL ROLE OF A YOUTH VOLLEYBALL COACH

The essential role of a youth volleyball coach goes beyond the boundaries of the court, extending into the realms of mentorship, leadership, and personal development. Coaches play a pivotal role in introducing young athletes to the intricacies of the game while simultaneously shaping their character and instilling core values. Beyond teaching the technicalities of passing and attacking, a coach serves as a guiding force, fostering teamwork, discipline, and a passion for continuous improvement. The impact of a coach goes far beyond wins and losses, influencing the growth of resilient, confident individuals who carry the lessons learned on the volleyball court into various aspects of their lives. In essence, a youth volleyball coach is not just a leader in the game but a mentor shaping young lives.

THE IMPACT OF COACHING ON YOUTH DEVELOPMENT

The impact of coaching on youth development in the context of volleyball is profound and far-reaching. Beyond honing athletic skills, a coach becomes a guiding force, instilling values such as teamwork, discipline, and resilience. Through the challenges and victories on the volleyball court, young athletes learn crucial life lessons, including goal-setting, team communication, and the importance of perseverance. A skilled coach not only imparts the technical aspects of the sport but also serves as a mentor, fostering a positive mindset and a strong work ethic. The nurturing environment created by a coach contributes significantly to the holistic development of youth, shaping them into well-rounded individuals equipped with the skills and attitudes necessary for success both in volleyball and in life.

SETTING THE FOUNDATION

In laying the foundation for coaching youth volleyball, the journey begins with a strategic blend of inspiration and organization. Coaches serve as architects, setting the stage for a season of development and growth. Establishing clear goals and conducting thoughtful team tryouts become the cornerstones, ensuring that each player's unique potential is recognized and celebrated. From instilling a love for the game to cultivating a positive team culture, this initial phase is pivotal. It's about more than teaching serves and attacks; it's about nurturing a passion for volleyball while building the fundamental skills and values that will shape young athletes both on and off the court. As coaches lay this groundwork, they become not only instructors but mentors, guiding the next generation toward a fulfilling and transformative volleyball experience.

ESTABLISHING SEASON GOALS

Establishing season goals in coaching youth volleyball is akin to charting a course for success. Coaches play a crucial role in crafting objectives that extend beyond wins and losses, focusing on the holistic development of young athletes. These goals serve as a guiding compass, shaping practice sessions and game strategies to align with broader aspirations. Whether it's fostering teamwork, improving individual skills, or instilling a sense of sportsmanship, the season's goals set the tone for a purposeful and enriching volleyball experience. By carefully articulating these objectives, coaches inspire players to reach beyond their limits, fostering a collective commitment to growth, camaraderie, and achievement throughout the season.

SEASON GOALS EXMPLES:

1. Develop proficient serving, passing, and spiking skills among players.
2. Foster a supportive team culture, emphasizing communication and camaraderie.
3. Instill values of sportsmanship, respect, and fair play within the team.
4. Encourage goal setting for both individual and team achievements.
5. Improve adaptability by adjusting strategies based on opponents and game dynamics.
6. Strive for consistent performance, minimizing errors throughout the season.
7. Enhance overall fitness and endurance to meet the demands of the game.
8. Cultivate leadership qualities among players, promoting initiative and teamwork.
9. Increase tactical understanding, focusing on formations, rotations, and strategic plays.
10. Nurture a genuine love for volleyball by creating a fun and positive team environment.
11. Prepare for competitive play by refining strategies and building mental resilience.
12. Tailor individual improvement plans, addressing specific areas of growth for each player.
13. Engage with the community, fostering a sense of responsibility and positive representation.
14. Achieve measurable milestones, such as a targeted win-loss ratio.
15. Foster a culture of continuous improvement through regular reflection and adaptation of strategies.

CONDUCTING SUCCESSFUL TEAM TRYOUTS

Conducting a successful team tryout in youth volleyball is an art that goes beyond assessing technical skills. It's about identifying potential, gauging coachability, and building a foundation for a cohesive team. Begin by creating a welcoming environment where players feel comfortable showcasing their abilities. A combination of skill assessments, drills, and scrimmage play provides a comprehensive view of each player's strengths and areas for improvement. However, don't overlook the intangibles—attitude, teamwork, and a willingness to learn are equally crucial. Communication is key; ensure players understand the evaluation process and provide constructive feedback. Ultimately, a successful tryout not only forms the basis of a talented team but also sets the tone for a season where growth, development, and the joy of playing volleyball are at the forefront.

COACHING FUNDAMENTALS

Coaching fundamentals in youth volleyball form the bedrock of a successful and impactful coaching journey. Beyond the technical intricacies of passing and attacking, effective coaching begins with a genuine passion for the sport and a deep commitment to fostering growth in young athletes. Establishing a positive and supportive environment is fundamental, where communication flows openly, and players feel motivated to push their boundaries. Coaches serve as mentors, guiding the development of fundamental skills while instilling values of teamwork, sportsmanship, and resilience. Successful coaching at the youth level involves not only teaching the game but also inspiring a love for volleyball that extends well beyond the confines of the court.

TEACHING FUNDAMENTAL VOLLEYBALL SKILLS

Here is a list of some of the Key Basic Fundamental Volleyball Skills:

1. **Serving:** Developing various serving techniques, including jump serves, float serves, and topspin serves.

2. **Setting:** Acquiring precise setting techniques to deliver accurate balls to teammates for effective attacks.

3. **Attacking/Spiking/Hitting:** Perfecting the approach, timing, and technique for powerful and accurate spikes at the net.

4. **Blocking:** Learning effective blocking strategies to defend against opponent spikes and disrupt their offensive plays.

5. **Digging (Defense):** Developing defensive skills to dig or receive opponent attacks, preventing them from scoring.

6. **Serve Receive:** Training to receive serves accurately, ensuring the ball is set up for effective offensive plays.

TEACHING FUNDAMENTAL VOLLEYBALL SKILLS
(SERVING)

Volleyball Float Serve:
1. Begin with a relaxed grip on the ball and stand with your feet shoulder-width apart with your non-htting side foot slightly in front.
2. With your Non-hitting hand, toss (lift) the ball slightly in front of you, allowing it to drop to your hitting hand.
3. Strike the ball with a flat, open hand using a quick and controlled motion.
4. Aim to contact the middle or bottom part of the ball to reduce spin, creating a unpredictable "floating" trajectory.
5. Follow through with your hitting hand finishing towards the zone you are aiming.

Volleyball Topspin Serve:
1. Adopt a similar stance to the float serve, but with a slight forward lean.
2. With your hitting hand, toss the ball a bit higher and slightly in front of you to allow for a downward striking motion.
3. Use a relaxed hand and wrist to generate topspin by contacting the top part of the ball.
4. The topspin will make the ball dip sharply so aim the trajectory slightly higher than the float and this will make it more challenging for opponents to receive.
5. Maintain good follow-through and focus on your serving target.

TEACHING FUNDAMENTAL VOLLEYBALL SKILLS
(SERVING)

Volleyball Jump Float Serve:

1. Start a few steps behind the baseline and take a short approach step before your jump.
2. Toss the ball higher with your non-hitting hand, allowing time for a powerful jump.
3. As you jump, keep your hitting arm back with and open palm.
4. Strike the ball with a strong, descending blow, aiming for the middle of the ball to generate power.
5. Land on both feet after the jump and quickly transition into your defensive position.

Volleyball Jump Topspin Serve:

1. Start a few steps behind the baseline and take a 3-step approach step before your jump.
2. Toss the ball higher (at least 2 times the players height) allowing time for a powerful jump.
3. As you jump, bring your hitting arm back, creating a whipping motion.
4. Strike the ball with a strong, descending blow, aiming for the top third of the ball to generate topspin and power.
5. Land on both feet after the jump and quickly transition into your defensive position.

TEACHING FUNDAMENTAL VOLLEYBALL SKILLS
(SETTING)

1. Ready Position:
• Assume an athletic stance with your feet shoulder-width apart with your right foot in slightly in front of the other..
• Bend your knees slightly to maintain quick movements.
• Position your hands above your forehead, forming a triangular shape with your thumbs and forefingers.

2. Hand Position:
• Create a comfortable but firm platform by bringing your hands together, fingers spread, and thumbs pointing down making a triangle shape with your fingers..
• Keep your wrists steady to provide stability for accurate sets.

3. Eye on the Ball:
• Focus on the ball as it approaches, tracking its speed, spin, and trajectory.
• Anticipate the ball's path to make precise decisions for setting.

4. Footwork:
• Position yourself under the ball by moving quickly and using small steps and get around the ball as you face the outside pin..
• Square your shoulders to the target (pin), ensuring a balanced and controlled setting position.
• Step with your right foot to the pin to initiate momentum and give you more power.

TEACHING FUNDAMENTAL VOLLEYBALL SKILLS
(SETTING)

5. Setting Techniques:
• Overhead Set (Hand Set): Use your fingertips to cushion the ball's impact and guide it accurately to your intended target.
• Overhead Push Set: Extend your arms fully, pushing the ball upward and forward with both hands for a quick and accurate set.

6. Setting Target:
• Aim for a position that allows the hitter to approach the ball comfortably.
• Set the ball precisely to the hitter's preferred hitting zone, considering their position and the defensive block.

7. Timing and Tempo:
• Coordinate with the hitter's approach, setting the ball at the right moment to optimize their hitting options.
• Vary the tempo of your sets to keep the opposing block and defense off-balance.

8. Communication:
• Verbally communicate with your teammates, indicating your intentions and calling for the ball.
• Establish non-verbal cues with your hitters to enhance understanding during the game.

TEACHING FUNDAMENTAL VOLLEYBALL SKILLS
(SETTING)

9. Creativity and Adaptability:
• Develop the ability to adapt to different situations, such as off-target passes or unexpected defensive plays.
• Use creativity in your sets, varying the height, speed, and spin to confuse the opposing team.

10. Continuous Practice:
• Regularly practice setting drills to refine your touch, accuracy, and decision-making skills.
• Work on setting from various positions on the court to enhance versatility.

Effective setting is crucial for a successful offensive play in volleyball. Consistent practice and a focus on technique will contribute to your proficiency as a setter on the team.

TEACHING FUNDAMENTAL VOLLEYBALL SKILLS
(ATTACKING)

1. Approach:
• Start your approach behind the 10ft line all dependent on your steps and if you are in system.
• Use a three-step or four-step approach, depending on personal preference and the play's speed.
- 3 step approach (outside hitter/right handed) - start with right foot
- 3 step approach (outside hitter/left handed) - start with left foot
- 3 step approach (opposite hitter/right handed) - start with right foot
- 3 step approach (opposite hitter/left handed) - start with left foot
- 4 step approach (outside hitter/right handed) - start with leftfoot
- 4 step approach (outside hitter/left handed) - start with right foot
- 4 step approach (opposite hitter/right handed) - start with left foot
- 4 step approach (opposite hitter/left handed) - start with right foot

2. Footwork:
• Coordinate your steps for an explosive jump, leading with your non-dominant foot.
• Maintain a quick and controlled footwork pattern, ensuring balance during the approach.

3. Arms and Hands:
• Swing your arms back during the approach, generating momentum for the jump.
• As you jump, bring your hitting arm back and your non-dominant arm up, preparing for the attack.

TEACHING FUNDAMENTAL VOLLEYBALL SKILLS
(ATTACKING)

4. Jump:
• Explode off both feet, reaching the peak of your jump at the ball's set point.
• Extend your hitting arm fully, reaching high above the net for optimal contact.

5. Contact Point:
• Strike the ball at the peak of your jump, ideally contacting it with the heel of your hand.
• Aim for the top of the ball to generate a downward trajectory with topspin and increase the chances of a successful attack.

6. Hitting Techniques:
• Power Hit (Spike): Swing your arm forcefully, snapping your wrist for power. Focus on hitting the ball down into the opponent's court.
• Roll Shot: Soften your hand and wrist, contacting the bottom of the ball to create a softer, controlled shot over the block.
• Tip/Dink: Gently redirect the ball with your fingertips, aiming for open spots on the opponent's side.

7. Targeting:
• Aim for open spaces on the opponent's side, targeting areas away from defenders.
• Adjust your attack based on the block and defensive positioning, opting for strategic shots.

TEACHING FUNDAMENTAL VOLLEYBALL SKILLS
(ATTACKING)

8. Follow-Through:
• Finish your attack with a complete follow-through, directing your hitting hand towards the target.
• Land on both feet, ready to transition to the defensive position.

9. Communication:
• Communicate with the setter and teammates, indicating your readiness to attack and calling for the set.
• Signal your intentions during the approach to maintain coordination.

10. Continuous Practice:
• Practice attacking from various positions on the court to adapt to different game situations.
• Work on your timing, jump height, and hitting techniques to enhance your attacking repertoire.

Regular practice and a focus on technique are essential for becoming a proficient attacker in volleyball. Consistency and adaptability will contribute to your effectiveness in scoring points for your team.

TEACHING FUNDAMENTAL VOLLEYBALL SKILLS
(BLOCKING)

1. Proper Starting Position: Emphasize players bending their knees slightly and lowering their hips as they start in an athletic stance (A.S.) as they stand square and even to the net with their elbows up parallel to the ground and hands open.

3. Proper Footwork: Practice Correct footwork to ensure players are quick and agile when moving laterally along the net for effective blocking.

- **1 Step** - In an A.S. take 1 step laterally then jump.
- **2 Step** - In an A.S. take 2 steps laterally then jump.
- **2 Step Crossover** - In an A.S., shift/turn your hips at 45 degrees, pivot on your leading foot, with bend arms swing and drive, then take a crossover step with your lagging foot across. Now take a step with your leading foot so that your body and hips are square again to the net then jump.
- **3 Step Crossover** - In an A.S., shift/turn your hips at 45 degrees, take a big steph with your leading foot, with bend arms swing and drive, then take a crossover step with your lagging foot across. Now take a step with your leading foot so that your body and hips are square again to the net then jump.
- **4 Step Shuffle Crossover** - In an A.S., take a 1 step lateral shuffle, then shift/turn your hips at 45 degrees, take a big steph with your leading foot, with bend arms swing and drive, then take a crossover step with your lagging foot across. Now take a step with your leading foot so that your body and hips are square again to the net then jump.

TEACHING FUNDAMENTAL VOLLEYBALL SKILLS
(BLOCKING)

3. Quick Reaction Time: Train players to react quickly to the opponent's movements by starting in an athletic stance (A.S.), enabling them to time their jumps and blocks effectively.

4. Penetrating the Net: Teach players to extend their arms penetrating the opponent's side to increase the chances of deflecting or blocking the ball and reaching over the net keeping their arms up until they hit the ground.

5. Reading the Setter: Develop skills in reading the opposing team's setter to anticipate the direction of the attack and position for a well-timed block.

6. Timing Jumps: Emphasize the importance of timing jumps correctly by reading the hitting (NOT the ball) as you watch them through the net to maximizing the blocking height and effectiveness.

7. Hand Positioning: Instruct players on proper hand positioning, focusing on forming a solid block with hands pressed over the net to minimize gaps. (BIG open hands and work on angles)

8. Eye Focus: Encourage players to keep their eyes on the ball and the opponent's hitting shoulder to anticipate the attack direction accurately.

TEACHING FUNDAMENTAL VOLLEYBALL SKILLS
(BLOCKING)

9. Communication: Foster effective communication between blockers, ensuring they coordinate their efforts to create a solid block and cover potential gaps. Have the pins say things like "Ready", "Ready", "Up!" OR "Ready", "Go!" to help.

10. Adaptability: Train players to adapt their blocking techniques based on the opponent's hitters, recognizing different attack styles and adjusting accordingly. Are they right or left handed?

11. Jumping Technique: Emphasize proper jumping technique, including explosive leg power and a coordinated arm swing with bent arms, to maximize height and reach during blocks.

12. Consistent Hand Pressure: Stress the importance of consistent hand pressure during the block, ensuring players maintain a strong and stable position at the net.

13. Land Safely: Teach players to land safely after a block, minimizing the risk of injuries and enabling them to recover quickly for the next play. Land on 2 feet!

14. Drills and Repetition: Incorporate blocking-specific drills into practices to provide ample opportunities for players to refine their blocking skills through repetition and reinforcement.

TEACHING FUNDAMENTAL VOLLEYBALL SKILLS
(DIGGING AND SERVE RECEIVE)

1. Ready Position:
• Stand with feet shoulder-width apart and knees slightly bent.
• Keep a low, athletic stance to facilitate quick movements.
• Position your arms in front of you with relaxed shoulders as you role your back, forming a passing platform with your arms.

2. Hand Position:
• Create a solid passing platform by clasping your hands together (one hand on top of the other), with your thumbs pointing downward.
• Keep your wrists firm, but not rigid, allowing for controlled movement.

3. Eye on the Ball:
• Focus on the approaching ball to your platform from the server or opponent's attack.
• Keep your eyes on the ball, tracking its movement to your platform anticipate its trajectory.

4. Angle and Direction:
• Angle your passing platform slightly upward, ensuring the ball travels towards the target.
• Adjust the platform's angle by dropping your shoulder to direct the ball to the intended setter or teammate.

5. Footwork:
• Move your feet to position yourself correctly in line with the ball's path.
• Use small, quick steps to adjust and maintain balance while passing.

6. Absorb the Force:
• Soften your elbows and shoulders to absorb the impact of the ball while maintaining the same angle, promoting a controlled rebound.
• Avoid locking your arms, as it can lead to less accurate passes.

7. Passing Techniques:
• Underhand Pass (Bump): Use the forearms to pass the ball in a controlled manner. Focus on a clean, direct contact.
• Overhead Pass (Set): Extend your arms above your head, using your firm hands in a triangle position using your fingertips to guide the ball accurately to the setter.

8. Communication:
• Verbally communicate with teammates to avoid confusion and ensure everyone knows their roles.
• Call for the ball if you are the intended passer or setter.

TEACHING FUNDAMENTAL VOLLEYBALL SKILLS
(DIGGING AND SERVE RECEIVE)

9. Anticipation and Reaction:
• Anticipate the opponent's play by reading their body language and positioning.
• React quickly to unexpected changes in the ball's trajectory.

10. Continuous Practice:
• Regularly practice passing drills to improve consistency, accuracy, and reaction time.
• Work on receiving various types of serves and attacks to develop a well-rounded skill set.

Remember, effective passing and receiving are fundamental skills in volleyball. Consistent practice and a focus on proper technique will contribute to your success on the court.

TIPS FOR EFFECTIVE COMMUNICATION

1. **Clear Verbal Communication:** Emphasize concise and clear verbal communication to convey information effectively during matches and practices.

2. **Positive Reinforcement:** Use positive reinforcement to acknowledge and celebrate good plays, fostering a motivating and supportive environment.

3. **Active Listening:** Encourage active listening among players to enhance understanding and responsiveness to instructions and feedback.

4. **Hand Signals:** Implement hand signals for quick and non-verbal communication, especially in noisy game environments.

5. **Encouraging Tone:** Maintain an encouraging and supportive tone, creating an atmosphere where players feel comfortable expressing themselves and asking questions.

6. **Pre-Game Meetings:** Conduct pre-game meetings to discuss strategies, set expectations, and ensure everyone is on the same page before stepping onto the court.

7. **Constructive Feedback:** Provide constructive feedback that focuses on improvement, offering specific guidance for skill enhancement without demotivating players.

TIPS FOR EFFECTIVE COMMUNICATION

8. **Timeout Discussions:** Utilize timeouts for brief and focused discussions, addressing challenges, adjusting strategies, and boosting team morale.

9. **Team Huddles:** Incorporate team huddles to reinforce unity, share insights, and boost motivation during critical moments in a match.

10. **Encourage Player Input:** Create an environment where players feel empowered to share ideas and contribute to strategic discussions.

11. **Non-Verbal Cues:** Incorporate non-verbal cues, such as eye contact or subtle gestures, to convey information without disrupting the flow of play.

12. **Individual Meetings:** Conduct individual meetings with players to discuss personal goals, concerns, and areas for improvement in a more private setting.

13. **Consistent Terminology:** Establish consistent and clear terminology for plays and strategies, reducing confusion and promoting quick understanding.

14. **Team-building Activities:** Integrate team-building activities to strengthen communication and foster camaraderie off the court.

15. **Post-Game Reviews:** Engage in post-game reviews to discuss performance, share insights, and collaboratively identify areas for improvement in future matches.

YOUTH VOLLEYBALL DRILLS

Embark on a dynamic journey of skill enhancement and team cohesion with these 25 volleyball drills outlined in this guide. Designed to elevate players' performance and foster a deeper understanding of the game, these drills encompass everything from fundamental techniques to some more advanced strategic maneuvers. Whether you're aiming to fine-tune serving precision, bolster defensive prowess, or enhance overall teamwork, these volleyball drills provide a comprehensive toolkit for coaches and players alike. Get ready to elevate your game and cultivate a winning spirit through purposeful and engaging training sessions.

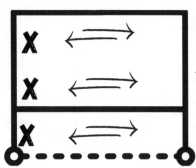

Drill: *Down and back skills*

Have each player grab a ball and pass to themselves as they walk from sideline to sideline. Then add setting and pass/set .

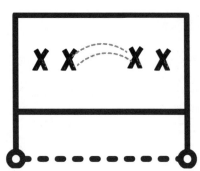

Drill: *Team Ball Control*

Make 2 lines and have 1 ball for the group. Have the first player pass the ball from 1 line to the other, then go to the back of the line on the other. Continuously players will pass, then move to each line. Try to see how many the group can do in a row.

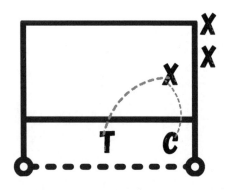

Drill: *Passing from toss – LB*

Have a group of players lined up and ready to go in at LB. Coach tosses the ball to the players facing you and they angle their platforms to the target. To make it more difficult, have them transition from base to defense. 5 balls each, then switch.

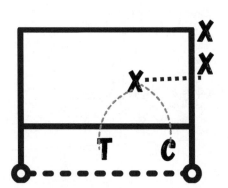

Drill: *Passing Movement from LB*

Have a line of players enter in defense at LB and shuffle inward. The coach will toss a ball and they will pass it to the target. Have them work on facing where the ball is coming from and angle towards the target. 5 balls each, then switch.

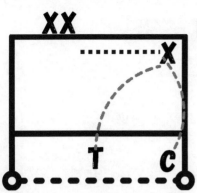

Drill: *Passing Movement – MB to line*

Have a line a players reach to go in MB. The coach will slap the ball and the players will run to the line, put their left foot on the line, and the coach will toss the ball. The player will dig the ball, angling their platform to the target. 5 balls per player, and switch.

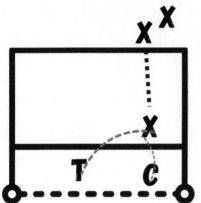

Drill: *Pass from endline*

Make a line of players at the endline. Have them shuffle up to the 10ft line as the coach tosses a ball. Have them work on keeping their shoulder square to the net and angling their platform to the target. 5 balls each, then switch

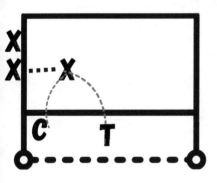

Drill: *Passing Movement from RB*

Players will make a line outside of RB. As coach slaps the ball, the player starting at defense will shuffle in facing the coach. Coach will toss the ball to the player as they angle their platform to the target. 5 balls each player, then switch.

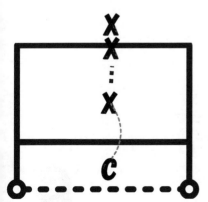

Drill: *MB run throughs*

Have all the players make a line in MB. Coach will toss a ball short and straight ahead so that the players learn to run through the ball and stay on their feet when possible as they pass back to the coach.

Drill: *Hitting Positions*

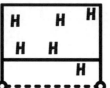

Have the team spread out on the court so they can work on hitting positions.

- **Position 1** - feet shoulder width apart, knees bent, arms back with palms up, and head up.
- **Position 2** - stand up with non-hitting arm up directed toward the direction they want to hit, hitting arm bent at the elbow with palm facing away, and chin up.
- **Position 3** - pull your non hitting arm into your mid-section, straighten/swing your hitting arm high, throw your relaxed wrist high as if was being thrown over the top of the ball.

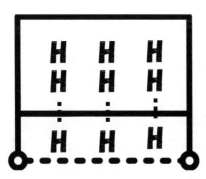

Drill: *Hitting Approach*

Just make 3-4 lines and have the hitters work on their hitting footwork approaches. 2-step, 3-step, and 4-step. Focus on throwing their arms back and the different hitting positions (Position 1, Position 2, and Position 3).

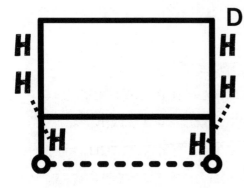

Drill: *Hitting Approach on Court*

Now have the players do their hitting approaches using the court. They should jump from outside the sideline and land on the inside of the court sideline. Once they approach on one line, have them rotated and go to the other line.

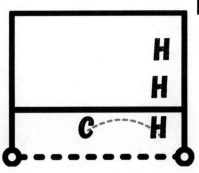

Drill: *Hitting lines from position 2*

Have a line of youth hitters ready to go in position 2 (non hitting arm up, and hitting arm elbow bent, up and open). Coach will toss the ball and the hitter will shuffle, make contact as they swing and finish in position 3 with their hand left up and a relaxed wrist (fingers pointing down).

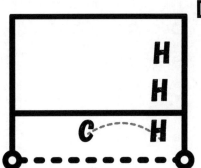

Drill: *Hitting lines from position 1*

Have a line of youth hitters ready to go in position 1 (arms back with palms up). Coach will toss the ball and the hitter will jump and hit position 2, then make contact as they swing and finish in position 3 with their hand left up and a relaxed wrist (fingers pointing down).

Drill: *Hitting lines –2 step*

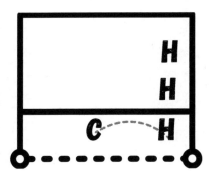

Have a line of youth hitters ready to go in running stance. If they are right-handed then their left foot should be forward, if they are left-handed then their right foot should be forward. The coach will toss a high ball off the net and the player will drop their hands back in position 1 immediately as they take their 2-step approach, then jump up and make contact with the ball finishing in position 3. If the players are ready then you can have them finish through with their swing.

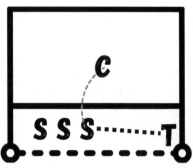

Drill: *Setting along the net*

Have a line of setters. Have the coach toss perfect balls to the setters so they can set to the target alongside the net

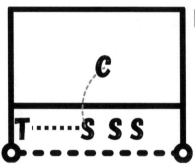

Drill: *Backsetting along the net*

Have a line of setters. Have the coach toss perfect balls to the setters so they can backset to the target alongside the net

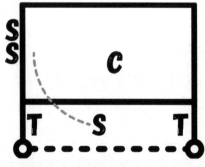

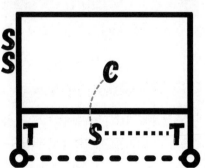

Drill: *Setting release drill*

Have a line of setters off the side, with one setter starting off at defense (or base if you want them to drop). Coach will slap the ball and the setter will release from defense to the net. The coach will then toss a perfect pass for the setter to either set in front or backset to a target behind them. Do about 10 each as you alternate 1 by 1 through.

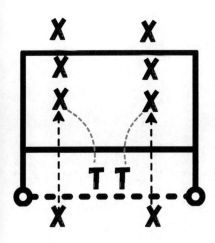

Drill: *Youth Serve Receive*

Make 2 lines. Have 1 step forward to hit a float ball over the net, another to become a tosser, and another to be the 1st passer. The server will serve a float ball right over the net to the passer in SR who will pass to the target. Have the passers work on holding their platform and dropping their inside should to the target. Passer becomes target, target becomes server, and server goes to the back of the passing line. Switch lines after 5 minutes so they can work on different angles and dropping their opposite shoulder.

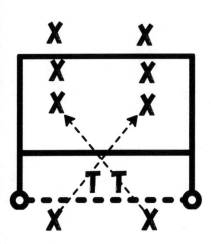

Drill: *Youth Serve Receive (cross)*

Make 2 lines. Have 1 step forward to hit a cross float ball over the net, another to become a tosser, and another to be the 1st passer. The server will serve a float ball cross right over the net to the passer in SR who will pass to the target. Have the passers face where the ball is coming from, then work on holding their platform and dropping their inside should to the target. Passer becomes target, target becomes server hitting cross, and server goes to the back of the passing line. Switch lines after 5 minutes so they can work on different angles and dropping their opposite shoulder.

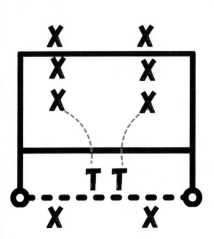

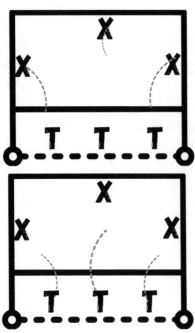

Drill: *Base to Defense digging (Perimeter)*

3 separate groups. Have each person start in base, move to defense and load. The tosser will toss the ball and the player will dig and catch their ball becoming the new toss, and tosser will go to the end of the line. Rotate positions after a couple of minutes.

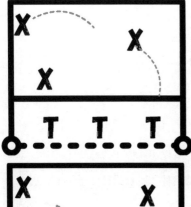

Drill: *Base to Defense digging (Rotation)*

3 separate groups. Have each person start in base, move to defense and load. The tosser will toss the ball and the player will dig and catch their ball becoming the new toss, and tosser will go to the end of the line. Rotate positions after a couple of minutes.

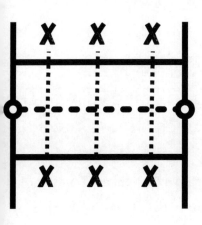

Drill: *Serving with partner*

Have players partner up and serve back and forth to one another on the court. The float serve would be a good starting serve. Talk about 1 foot in front of the other, tossing with their non hitting hand, making firm contact on the middle of the ball, and finishing to the target. Step back to make it more difficult.

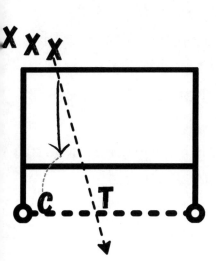

Drill: *Serve and Dig*

Have all players make a line. Have them serve 1 at a time, then immediately run to base, where the coach or another tosser will toss a ball for them to dig to a target.

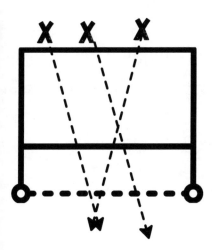

Drill: *Serving Consitency*

Have all players grab a ball a see how many serves they can get out of 10. Just have them retry and try again each time trying to beat their previous score. Once they get all 10 in a row, now see how many in a row they can get and try setting a high team and individual score.

Drill: *Serving Relay Game*

starting position

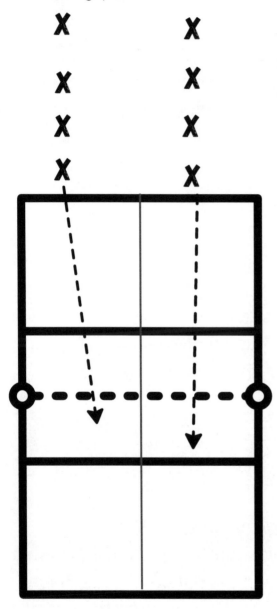

Split the team up into 2 teams and have those teams make 2 lines. The first person in each line will have a ball. On count, have them serve. If they miss their serve, then they will have to retrieve their ball and come back to the line to serve again. If they get their serve OVER the net and in, then they will go run and get their ball and hand it to the person in line who will then serve. Once everyone has served the ball over the net and the last person cross the line, then that team wins.

Here are some ways to adjust:
- If someone misses their 1st 3 servers, then they can take 2 steps up.
- Even out the teams so that you have strong and weak servers in both.
- Add zones to make it more difficult if needed.

VOLLEYBALL FORMATIONS

In the sport of volleyball there are 6 players related to 6 positions on the court. We represent this in the box below:

4	**3**	**2**
5	**6**	**1**

Before the ball is served by any side, no one can overlap their position with either a person to the side or in front or behind them. Now it does NOT affect players catty corner from them.

So if we look at position 1. Position 1 only needs to NOT overlap with 2 or 6, but can overlap with any one else including 3.

This works with the other positions on the court as well. So as we take in account these positions in serve and serve receive, we only avoid the overlap of the directly touching (to side, front, and behind) positions before the ball is served.

UNDERSTANDING THE 6-2 FORMATION

HOW MANY SETTERS? 2
HOW MANY HITTERS? 6
WHAT DOES THIS MEAN?

During all 6 rotations you will always have a setter in backrow and 3 hitters always in the front.

UNDERSTANDING THE 6-2 FORMATION

ADVANTAGES

- Easy to learn system and great for development.
- Multiple attackers to help spread the offense as you always have 3 in the front row.
- Maintain height at the net if you have small setters.
- It's very adaptable and can be easily transitioned to a 5-1 if needed.
- You can have smaller setters as they don't play front row.
- You can match up the setters with their hitters for more consistency.

DISADVANTAGES

- Frequent substitutions.
- No front row setter, so it's difficult to defend overpasses.
- No front row setter, so NO offensive hitting from setter as they are back row.
- Lot of movement for setters which can make it difficult to transition.
- Setters need to play defense all 6 rotations, so you need setters that are quick and can dig the ball.

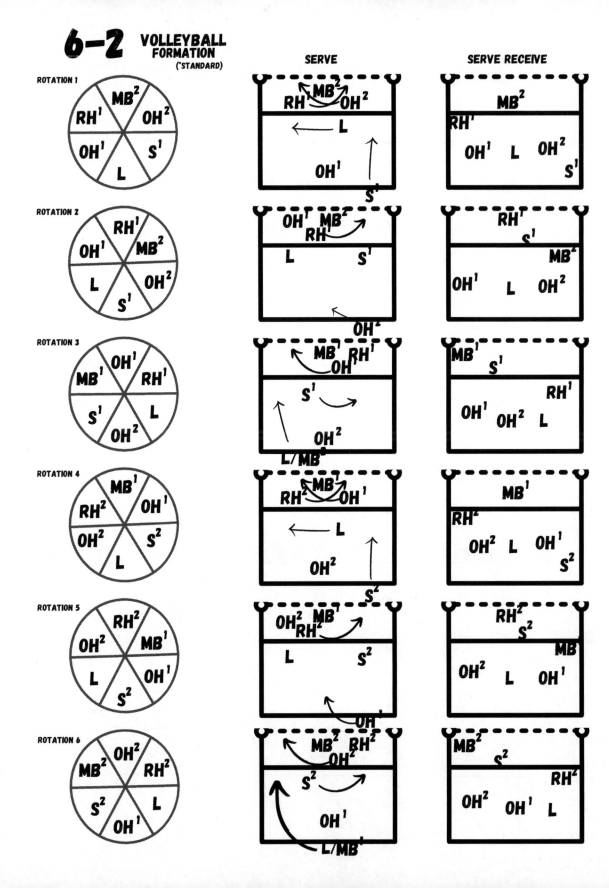

HOW MANY SETTERS? 6
HOW MANY HITTERS? 6
WHAT DOES THIS MEAN?

This is a youth volleyball formation which lets every player who plays right back get an opportunity to set which always leaves 3 hitters in the front row.

EXPLORING THE 6-6 FORMATION

ADVANTAGES

- Great development system for you players as everyone gets to learn most if NOT all positions on the court.
- Everyone gets to be an attacker.
- Everyone gets to be a setter.

DISADVANTAGES

- No consistency in setting as everyone rotation it's someone different.
- No consistency in attackers as everyone gets a chance to become a hitter in front row.
- You are NOT playing at the team's strengths as everyone is moving around.

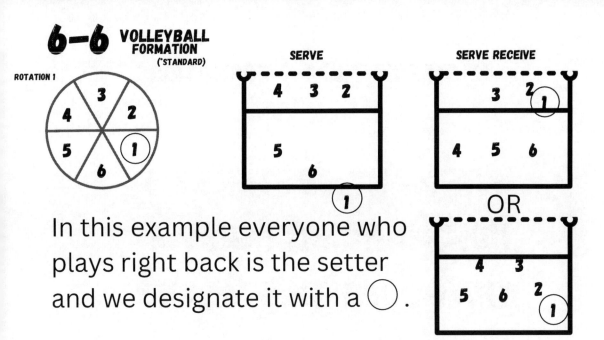

6-6 VOLLEYBALL FORMATION
(*STANDARD*)

ROTATION 1

SERVE

SERVE RECEIVE

OR

In this example everyone who plays right back is the setter and we designate it with a ⃝ .

There are many ways to accomplish these rotations so we will be general. You only need to know 1 rotation and that's rotation 1 of a standard 6-2 (of course you can try this in other rotations, but this is easier to learn and is a great learning experience for setters transitioning). As you rotate players after a side out, the new right back player is the new setter and everyone else changes positions as well. You can always designate positions such as certain people could always play MH in front row to customize it to fit your need.

HOW MANY SETTERS? 6
HOW MANY HITTERS? 4
WHAT DOES THIS MEAN?

This is a youth volleyball formation that's perfect for the young kids which allows every person who is right front to be the setter. There will always be just 2 hitters in front row for every rotation.

MASTERING THE 4-6 FORMATION

ADVANTAGES

- Everyone gets to set. Great for development.
- Easy for youth teams to start learning about positions and transitioning as a hitter.

DISADVANTAGES

- No consistency with setter as everyone is setting.
- Typically, no specialization as everyone is playing multiple positions.

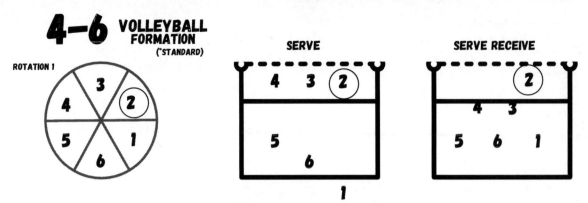

In this example everyone who plays right front is the setter and we designate it with a ◯ .

There are many ways to accomplish these rotations so we will be general. You only need to know 1 rotation and that's rotation 6 of a standard 5-1 (again, you can try other rotations to fill your need but this should be the easiest as the setter does little movement which is great for young players). As you rotate players at side out, the new right front player is the new setter and everyone else changes positions as well. You can always designate positions such as certain people could always play MH in front row to customize it to fit your need.

STRATEGIC GAME PLAY

Youth volleyball strategic gameplay is a dynamic blend of skill, coordination, and tactical finesse while still maintaining a sense of development. Coaches and players alike delve into formulating effective game plans that go beyond individual prowess, emphasizing cohesive teamwork and placing individuals in the correct positions for them to succeed on the court. Understanding various formations, such as the 6-2, 6-6, and 4-6, becomes paramount in optimizing player positions and rotations. These strategic formations not only dictate offensive strategies but also influence defensive setups, creating a well-rounded approach to the game. Ultimately, youth volleyball is about development and making players better, so still keep that in focus as you develop a strategic plan.

TIPS TO FORMULATING GAME PLANS

1. **Player Development Focus:** Prioritize individual skill development within the game plan. Tailor strategies that allow players to showcase and enhance their unique strengths, contributing to both personal growth and team success.

2. **Positional Congruence:** Ensure that players are placed in positions that align with their skill sets and strengths. This not only optimizes individual performance but also fosters a sense of confidence and competence within the team.

3. **Positive Reinforcement:** Infuse the game plan with positivity. Acknowledge and celebrate players' achievements, both big and small, fostering a constructive and uplifting team environment that encourages continuous improvement.

TIPS TO FORMULATING GAME PLANS

4. **Clear Communication:** Emphasize effective communication as a fundamental element of the game plan. Ensure players understand their roles, responsibilities, and how they fit into the overall strategy. Open lines of communication contribute to seamless execution on the court.

5. **Adaptability:** Instill flexibility within the game plan, allowing for adjustments based on the flow of the match and the strengths and weaknesses observed in the opposing team. Teaching adaptability prepares players for dynamic situations and enhances their strategic thinking.

6. **Encourage Team Cohesion:** Develop plays that promote teamwork and collaboration. Emphasize the importance of synchronized movements, coordinated plays, and mutual support among teammates to maximize the effectiveness of the game plan.

TIPS TO FORMULATING GAME PLANS

7. **Goal Setting:** Incorporate short-term and long-term goals within the game plan. Establishing achievable milestones provides players with a sense of direction and purpose, motivating them to continuously strive for improvement.

8. **Strategic Timeouts:** Utilize timeouts strategically to provide feedback, make adjustments, and offer encouragement. These breaks not only allow for tactical discussions but also serve as moments to maintain a positive team spirit during challenging situations.

9. **Focus on Sportsmanship:** Emphasize good sportsmanship as an integral part of the game plan. Reinforce the importance of respect for opponents, officials, and teammates, creating a positive atmosphere that transcends competition.

10. **Celebrate Effort:** Recognize and celebrate the effort and hard work put in by players. Encourage a growth mindset where mistakes are viewed as opportunities to learn, fostering resilience and a continual desire to improve within the framework of the game plan.

VOLLEYBALL DEFENSE

When it comes to deciding on a defense, a crucial realization is that it's not always about stopping every attack your opponents throw at you; it's about making calculated decisions as a team. You'll find that there are attacks you can take away with a well-executed defense, but in doing so, you might concede openings in other areas. It's a strategic dance, a give-and-take, where the team must assess their strengths and the opponent's weaknesses, adapting their defensive formations and tactics accordingly. In this book we are going to go over the most common volleyball defense in volleyball and that is the Perimeter (or Perimeter "Hybrid" in some cases)

PRINCIPLES OF PERIMETER "HYBRID" DEFENSE

In a volleyball perimeter hybrid defense with the off blocker picking up tips, the back-row players are strategically positioned near the back boundary of the court to guard against deep attacks. The off blocker, typically one of the front-row players, is responsible for reading and reacting to "tips" or short, finesse shots executed by the opposing team. This defensive formation ensures that both powerful hits and subtle tips are accounted for, allowing the team to maintain effective coverage of the backcourt.

PRINCIPLES OF PERIMETER "HYBRID" DEFENSE

ADVANTAGES

1. Effective Against Short Shots: The presence of the off blocker in the front row enhances the defense's ability to handle short and finesse shots like tips, dumps, and roll shots effectively.

2. Balanced Front and Back Coverage: This defense provides a balanced approach by combining the strengths of perimeter back-row defense with added coverage near the net, making it adaptable to various attack types.

3. Seamless Transition to Offense: With a front-row player prepared to defend against tips, quick transitions from defense to offense are facilitated, as they can use their position to set up offensive plays.

ADVANTAGES (CONT.)

4. Diverse Defensive Options: The off blocker can contribute to both blocking and digging, adding versatility to the defense and making it effective against different attacking styles.

5. Reduced Vulnerability to Short Attacks: The combination of back-row and front-row players reduces the vulnerability to short attacks, as there's a player strategically placed to defend against them.

6. Improved Net Presence: Having a front-row player ready to pick up tips or block attacks can increase the team's overall presence at the net, making it harder for the opposing team to execute effective offensive plays.

PRINCIPLES OF PERIMETER "HYBRID" DEFENSE

DISADVANTAGES

1. Holes in Defense: The off blocker's transition from the front row to the back row may leave gaps in the defense, especially around their base.

2. Increased Pressure on Back-Row Players: The back-row players, including the off blocker transitioning to the back row, face increased pressure to cover both deep shots and holes around the off blocker's base.

3. Dependence on the Off Blocker's Skill: The effectiveness of this defense relies heavily on the off blocker's ability to read the game, anticipate attacks, and react swiftly.

DISADVANTAGES (CONT.)

4. Transition Challenges: The transition from a off blocking position to transitional attacking position for the off blocker after picking up a tip can be intricate and may not always be executed seamlessly, leaving 1 less hitter.

5. Potential for Miscommunication: Defending shots in the vicinity of the off blocker's base may require clear communication between players to avoid overlaps or gaps.

6. Predictability: Skilled opponents may recognize that shots are likely to target the off blocker's base in this defense.

PERIMETER HYBRID DEFENSE

Base (standard lineup):

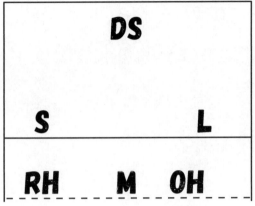

We are going to start in a standard base with setter back row. Don't release from base until the ball leaves the setters hands. The off blockers will move in more for tips in this defense.

Defense against...

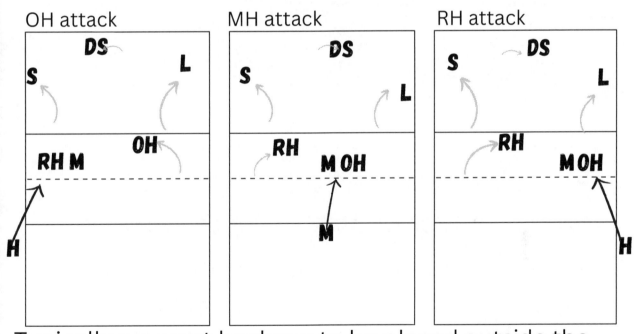

Typically we want backrow to be placed outside the block & between the block. If the block is closed then instead of between the block, then BR can read. Usually never behind the block.

KEY CONCEPTS: SEEMS

One of the key concepts of the backrow defense is who's ball is it and who has what on the seem?:

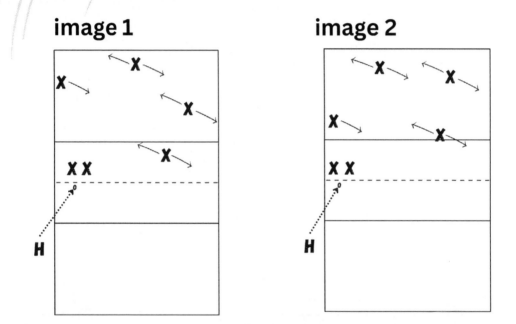

In this example, it's typical for middle back to cover behind and the corners, but if you are blocking line and middle back moves over into the seem of the block in image 2, then you might have to make some adjustments on who has what seem.

KEY CONCEPTS: READING

The next key concept is reading around the block to set up your back row defense.

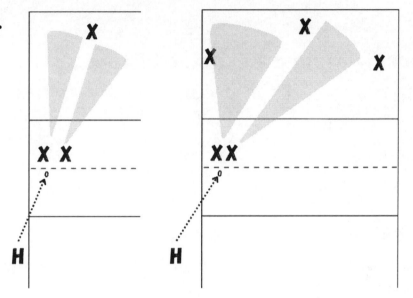

The key is for any back row defender is to move to their defensive position and stop before the hitter makes contact. As far as position, you never what to be behind the block, as you want to be able to see the hitter and get around the block as those are the hard hits and you want to be in position before they are hit.

KEY CONCEPTS: BLOCKING

The next key concept is blocking (line, cross, and ball).

Blocking against a Outside hitter. :

line	cross	ball

 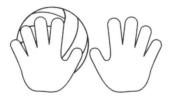 

Blocking against a typical Rightside hitter. :

line   cross   ball

For blocking line, make sure you place your hand on the inside of the court to the ball. For cross, your outside hand should be on the ball. And for ball, both hands should be on the ball.

NAVIGATING CHALLENGES

Navigating challenges in coaching youth volleyball demands a blend of resilience, adaptability, and a steadfast commitment to player development. From addressing individual skill gaps to managing team dynamics, challenges come in various forms. Coaches serve as mentors, guiding players through setbacks and instilling a mindset that embraces learning from failures. Balancing the diverse skill levels and personalities within the team requires a delicate touch, fostering an environment where players feel supported and encouraged to overcome obstacles. Successful coaches understand that challenges are not roadblocks but opportunities for growth, both for the individual athletes and the team as a whole. By navigating these challenges with patience, insight, and a focus on continuous improvement, coaches play a pivotal role in shaping not just skilled volleyball players, but resilient and confident individuals.

TIPS TO NAVIGATING CHALLENGES IN YOUTH VOLLEYBALL

1. **Open Communication:** Encourage open and honest communication with players to understand their concerns, aspirations, and challenges.

2. **Adaptability**: Be flexible and adapt strategies to address evolving challenges, whether they are related to skill development, team dynamics, or external factors.

3. **Individualized Support:** Recognize that each player is unique. Provide individualized support to address specific challenges and foster personal growth.

4. **Positive Reinforcement:** Emphasize positive reinforcement to boost morale during difficult times. Celebrate small victories and progress.

5. **Team Building:** Foster a sense of unity and camaraderie within the team. Team-building activities can strengthen bonds and improve overall resilience.

6. **Goal Setting:** Collaboratively set achievable goals with players, providing a roadmap for overcoming challenges and measuring success.

7. **Mentorship**: Establish a mentorship culture within the team where experienced players can support and guide newer or struggling teammates.

8. **Constructive Feedback**: Offer constructive feedback that focuses on improvement rather than criticism, creating a culture of continuous learning.

9. **Patience:** Understand that progress takes time. Demonstrate patience and perseverance to inspire players during challenging phases.

10. **Conflict Resolution:** Address conflicts promptly and constructively, promoting a positive team environment where challenges become opportunities for growth.

11. **Empowerment:** Empower players to take ownership of their development. Encourage them to actively seek solutions to challenges and contribute to team strategies.

12. **Wellness Focus:** Prioritize the physical and mental well-being of players. A healthy and positive environment can help overcome various challenges.

13. **Continuous Learning:** Model a growth mindset by embracing challenges as learning opportunities. Demonstrate the importance of ongoing improvement for both coaches and players.

14. **Celebrate Resilience:** Acknowledge and celebrate resilience in the face of challenges. Recognize the effort and determination displayed by players, reinforcing their commitment to personal and team growth.

TIPS TO ADDRESS INDIVIDUAL AND TEAM ISSUES

1. **Open Communication:** Establish transparent communication channels to address concerns and issues promptly.

2. **Individual Meetings:** Conduct one-on-one meetings with an additional adult on hand with players to understand their perspectives and challenges.

3. **Active Listening:** Practice active listening to empathize with individual concerns and foster trust within the team.

4. **Conflict Resolution**: Develop conflict resolution strategies to address interpersonal issues and maintain a harmonious team environment.

5. **Constructive Feedback:** Provide constructive feedback with a focus on improvement, emphasizing the positive aspects of each player's performance.

6. **Team-Building Activities:** Integrate team-building activities to strengthen relationships and build camaraderie among players.

7. **Leadership Development:** Encourage leadership qualities within the team to promote peer support and collaborative problem-solving.

TIPS TO ADDRESS INDIVIDUAL AND TEAM ISSUES

8. **Goal Alignment:** Ensure that individual and team goals are aligned, fostering a collective sense of purpose and unity.

9. **Performance Plans:** Develop personalized performance plans for players, addressing specific areas of improvement based on individual needs.

10. **Mentorship Program:** Establish a mentorship program where experienced players provide guidance and support to teammates facing challenges.

11. **Encourage Self-Reflection:** Promote self-reflection among players to encourage personal responsibility and awareness of their contributions to team dynamics.

12. **Team Discussions:** Facilitate open team discussions to address collective challenges and collaboratively devise solutions.

13. **Positive Reinforcement:** Emphasize positive reinforcement to celebrate successes, both individual and team-related.

14. **Adaptability:** Be flexible and adaptive in coaching strategies, recognizing that different players may require varied approaches to address their issues.

15. **Wellness Check-ins:** Conduct regular wellness check-ins to ensure the mental and emotional well-being of players and address any issues affecting their performance.

MANAGING PLAYER AND PARENT EXPECTATIONS

Managing player and parent expectations in youth volleyball is a delicate balancing act that contributes significantly to the overall success and enjoyment of the season. For players, setting realistic and achievable goals fosters a sense of purpose and direction. Coaches play a crucial role in communicating these expectations clearly and **early** , emphasizing individual improvement, teamwork, and the joy of playing the sport. Encouraging open dialogue with players allows coaches to address concerns and align expectations effectively. On the parental front, transparency is key. Establishing clear communication channels helps manage expectations regarding playing time, skill development, and team dynamics. Regular updates on player progress and emphasizing the developmental aspect of youth sports contribute to a positive parent-coach partnership. By fostering a collaborative and supportive environment, coaches can ensure that both players and parents share realistic expectations, leading to a more fulfilling and successful youth volleyball experience for everyone involved.

SEASON MANAGEMENT

Season management in youth volleyball is a comprehensive orchestration of planning, guidance, and celebration. Coaches navigate the intricacies of organizing practices, coordinating game schedules, and ensuring the holistic development of each player. From setting season goals to refining strategies, effective management involves a keen understanding of the team's dynamics and individual strengths. Beyond the court, coaches play a crucial role in fostering a positive team culture, managing player and parent expectations, and instilling values of sportsmanship. As the season unfolds, the coach's ability to adapt, motivate, and celebrate milestones contributes to a fulfilling and transformative experience for young athletes. Season management in youth volleyball is not just about winning games; it's about shaping resilient individuals who carry the lessons learned on the court into their lives beyond the season.

REFLECTIONS ON THE SEASON AND FUTURE PLANNING

Reflection on the season and future planning in youth volleyball marks a crucial juncture for coaches. As the season concludes, coaches assess the team's progress, identifying areas of success and opportunities for growth. Thoughtful reflection goes beyond wins and losses, encompassing the development of individual players and the team as a whole. These insights pave the way for future planning, allowing coaches to refine strategies, set new goals, and adapt training approaches. The process involves not only evaluating performance on the court but also considering the overall impact on the players' character, teamwork, and love for the sport. As coaches look to the future, the aim is not just to create skilled athletes but to cultivate well-rounded individuals prepared for the next chapter of their volleyball journey.

RESOURCES FOR COACHES

BOOKS AND WEBSITES

Volleyballtools.com
(Get FREE line up sheets, libero tracking sheets, scouting sheets, & more!)

Books:

VOLLEYBALL GAME STATS
ATTACKING SHEET EXAMPLE

VOLLEYBALL GAME STATS
PASSING SHEET EXAMPLE

VOLLEYBALL SIMPLE
SCOUTING SHEET

VOLLEYBALL PRACTICE PLAN
SHEET

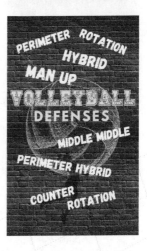

CONCLUSION

In the final chapter of "Coaching Youth Volleyball," we celebrate the incredible journey of mentorship, skill development, and camaraderie that defines the world of coaching young athletes. As coaches, we've explored the intricacies of teaching fundamental skills, designing effective drills, and formulating strategic game plans. Beyond the wins and losses, this book has underscored the profound impact coaches have on shaping the character, resilience, and sportsmanship of the next generation. Whether you're a seasoned coach or a newcomer to the sport, may this guide serve as a lasting resource, empowering you to inspire, guide, and foster the holistic development of young athletes. As we conclude, let's revel in the shared victories, the lessons learned, and the enduring passion ignited within the hearts of both coaches and players alike. The journey continues, and the impact of coaching resonates far beyond the volleyball court.

Made in United States
Troutdale, OR
11/18/2024

25033549R00042